HEART STONES

James Nash was born in London in 1949, and has been a resident of Leeds since 1971. He is a well-known provider of creative writing workshops in schools, universities and the community, and is regularly called on as a host of literary events. His collections include *A Bench For Billie Holiday: 70 Sonnets* (2018), and *Cinema Stories* (2015, with Matthew Hedley Stoppard), both published by Valley Press.

Heart Stones

JAMES NASH

Valley Press

First published in 2021 by Valley Press
Woodend, The Crescent, Scarborough, YO11 2PW
www.valleypressuk.com

ISBN 978-1-912436-64-4
Cat. no. VP0185

Cover and text design by Peter Barnfather.
Illustrations by Jacky Fleming.
Edited by Jo Brandon.

Printed and bound in the EU by Pulsio, Paris.

Contents

Yorkshire skies for Patricia

We shared these Yorkshire skies at different times,
A West Riding jumble of spire and mill
And, much later, the eastern coastal dreams
Which began for me at Garrowby Hill.
I'd no idea fifty years ago
That each daily walk would now be full of you,
The cliffs and beaches, where white pebbles glow,
Each prospect of the Wolds, each distant view.
And yesterday I saw across the bay
As dusk deepened with the slow dropping sun,
You signalling in the last dregs of day;
You are the lighthouse flash, not yet quite done.
I would give you a heart-stone from the beach
But you are fading light, too faint to reach.

Introduction

For the past ten years or so I have lived between a city, Leeds, and the small seaside town of Bridlington in the East Riding of Yorkshire. Both places have assumed a huge importance in my life. Leeds has been my home for fifty years since I began an MA in English and Anglo-Irish literature in 1971. The stones and statues of the city, the parks and green spaces, are all part of me. Yorkshire stone and my bones are one.

Bridlington with its beautiful coastline and surrounding countryside, much celebrated by David Hockney, has assumed an equal importance. The names of birds, wild-flowers and butterflies, forgotten since childhood, have come back to me. I have become aware of the changes to the seasons in a way that city-living can be more be-grudging of.

The title of this collection comes from a celebration of city stones, and of seaside fossils, shells and pebbles. In one, buses lumber up Headingley Lane past the repurposed, gritstone mansions of nineteenth-century manufacturing tycoons, in the other, tractors pull ploughs across fields close to cliff edges turning over the chalky stones that are an integral part of the soil.

I would like to thank my partner David Robinson for his gift of heart-shaped pebbles on our beach rambles, the anonymous boy on the bike who made the massive out-line of a heart from large white stones at South Landing, and artist Jacky Fleming whose pictures and drawings both found the essence of my poems and gave me fresh inspiration in their turn.

As I have written before sometimes poems start living when one reads them aloud. Sonnets, thick with rhymes and iambic pentameter, respond and come to life off the page particularly well.

James Nash, 2021

Heart stones

I

The incoming tide has covered them, fanned
Over, drowned the heart-shaped pattern of stones
Made from beach pebbles and secured in sand.
Large, white punctuation marks; the bleached bones
Of a dinosaur's toes, gathered, arranged
By a young artist on a bike with time
He did not have, until all slowed and changed,
To leave temporary signs in chalky rhyme.
From our cliff top eyrie we see it all,
Huge heart under water unmoved by tide.
Can love survive whatever might befall,
Perhaps live on when other things have died?
Just this; in slow erosion, it is worn
Down, dissolving more each day, stone by stone.

My jacket is weighted with all the stones
You give me when we walk along the shore,
Not heavy, more like a trove of old coins
Left by the tide: and I love them even more
Because you gave them and maybe I think
When I am away from these eastern seas
I'll be reassured by their heavy clink
And the memories held by each of these.
So, spring has come to the Wolds, see it light
The hawthorn with the sharp of acid green,
The fields are frost after a clear, cold night,
Birds wheel as one to a rhythm unseen
And in my pockets like the rising sap
Pebble hearts clatter with soft hammer tap.

Miniaturist

I have become a miniaturist
For these times, larger, more expansive views
Forsaken for a closer look. The list
Of plants and flowers I examine grows.
Butterflies and fossils, bees and then snails,
Dew on grass, bent already with their seeds,
Each small, perfect universe never fails
To lift me, it nourishes, slakes and feeds.
When I scan the tiny speedwell flower,
Its blue startling against the cliff-side grass,
Makes a slowed-down world seem even slower,
And celebrates each second as they pass.
May I always be this clear microscope,
Where miracles of detail bring me hope.

Fossil

In some future fossil world might I be
A knucklebone caught in a chalky cliff,
Left behind by a slow-retreating sea,
The old stars burning, would it seem enough?
Here on our Jurassic coast we have found
Occasional trapped shellfish calcified
By a million years of weight, the grind
Of rocks and sand left by an ancient tide.
But if I'm that bone someone comes upon,
Takes home in a pocket, there may be grace
In the explosion when this world is done,
Silica into the Architect's face,
Flicked by a finger from her godly eye,
A scatter of stars in a different sky.

Shell

If this had been my home, this pearly cave,
This tiny butter dish, this geometry
Of something close to bone, I would not leave
Its cool construction, placement by the sea.
But it is empty, its nacreous shine
Is the sad glossiness of ghostly gone.
Nothing clings to it, just the faintest sign
That something lived here, something called this home.
And now it seems that simple bi-valve life
Has much to like and much to recommend,
An intense belonging, perhaps too brief;
Humans may find it hard to understand.
Being broken open (then nothing more)
Food for an oystercatcher on the shore.

Stone

The stone is small, studded with tiny shells
Of long dead creatures who clutched hard their home
Under the water, broken limestone bells
That housed them once but now can have no claim
To life at all, just the treasure of one
Dog walker's beachcombings that demonstrate
Chalky memorials to a time long gone,
It sits on the table, unmoving, mute
But I take on its story, stand near
As if I might sense what happened somehow,
The maritime journey that brought it here,
The ebb of long-gone tides, their tugging flow;
And it's my barnacled heart that I see
Broken yet unbroken. Hard-calloused. Me.

Extinct

Sometimes I cycle home a different way
Through this city that I have loved so long
As if to take it by surprise, and see
An older side, and hear a distant song.
This used to be a town of striking clocks
That sounded the quarters, the halves and hours,
Newspaper sellers sold their wares to flocks
And bands of shoppers, and there were flowers
Too. Rag and bone men rattled down the street
But now the city seems almost swept clean
The informal history I used to meet,
Extinct, no longer witnessed, no longer seen.
Perhaps one day I'll take a corner fast
And ambush a Leeds I thought was past.

Apollo

He is unresisting, thrust in the car,
Curly head against the passenger seat,
The dog sneaks up closer though not too near
Perhaps there is still strength to the sun god's heat.
Moving Apollo is not done with ease
His wattage much dimmed but still to be felt
What's the health and safety, the legalese
Of god-moving, to belt or not to belt?
In the end he effects the transition
Between the Yorkshires, imperturbably
Taking up a commanding position,
Stone profile displayed, with eyes that don't see.
Who knows the journeys that he has taken,
Chipped and cracked but in the end unbroken.

The Head

For forty years a carved and bearded face
Has been the keystone over my front door,
Its stony gaze has not the slightest trace
Of warmth and humour, but it is worth more
As it holds the door arch inviolate.
Such metaphors figured in my life,
Certain key balances of strength and weight
Have upheld the structure, kept me safe.
They might be kindness, even love perhaps,
They change, I've sometimes kept abreast of them
And found the words for them upon my lips,
But now for a symbol I can call my own:
A seabird, outstretched wings drying in the sun
After cold sea fishing, may be the one.

Victoria

Famously unamused, she sits and stares
Across Woodhouse Lane to a distant hill,
Her plinth so high, I wonder how she fares,
Her present location a bitter pill;
She once sat outside Leeds Town Hall and reigned
Over the city-centre, then came the move
To the park, her expression slightly strained
Watching youngsters experiment with love.
For me she is where she has always been,
Passing on my bike or the bus I spy
A touch of mossy damp, she is bright green,
With only pigeons to meet her chilly eye.
Oh Vicky, old love, may I call you this?
Stony retirement does not look like bliss.

Lions
(and some bad rhyming)

Shabby beasts sat guarding the old Town Hall,
Staring straight ahead, heraldic and strong,
British Lions couchant, they say it all;
Queen and country always first, right or wrong.
Just lately I sense a left-leaning bent
From one who fixes a quizzical eye
Over what is going on, more than a glint
Of cynicism for that old 'do or die'.
The other keeps politics close to his chest,
Has money perhaps in offshore accounts,
Thinks the country is down the drain, gone west,
Sees a bleeding heart and wants to pounce.
Victorians both, some things make them wince,
Like the Henry Moore on its nearby plinth(ce).

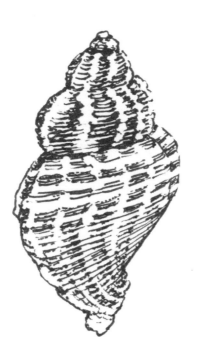

Beliefs and borrowings

My head and heart are full of others' lines
That sing in me to frame and shape my thought.
Forgive the borrowings, each one defines
The haunting by others' ghosts, unsought.
And if the words used in each humble piece
Can sometimes echo a more brilliant soul,
Forgive my scavenging heart to release
Me from what I owe, any unpaid bill.
For in these words I battle with belief,
With mysteries of living and of death.
Forgive me, a borrowing, light-fingered thief,
Who breathes in the air then shares others' breath.
And if you like my words, forgive my flaws
And jackdaw pilfering, these lines are yours.

Writing desk

I change rooms, escape sounds of saw and drill
Move to a table in a window space,
Old and battered, it carries with it still
A Georgian simplicity, the grace
Of past elegance, a view of garden,
Clear the plants, set out my laptop, gaze out
To roses and lupins in abandon,
To a busy road, folk walking about.
And then I see beneath its glossy shine
And find the inky depths of spill and stain
For this was a desk in another time,
And my kinship to it becomes more plain.
I sit where others sat and thought and wrote,
Heir to what caught their mind, and clutched their throat.

Winifred Holtby, Rudston:
A sixteen line sonnet, by accident

Her family house behind these high walls,
A brass plaque on the gatepost tells me so.
I am a pilgrim, cycling through these hills,
The awkward reverence I feel, I know
Owes something to Larkin, others too,
Crowd through my mind as I take in the place
Where her fire began, her genius grew.
I'm a beehive of quotation, a race
Of water from the Wolds down to the sea
Where trout and grayling splash and hide;
Sometimes I see them flicker as they flee
My gaze, showing a coppery side.
And she was such a one, she shone bright
In southern cities for a little time
Creating a lamp of imagined light
In words that showed the Riding of her home.

Taxonomy

I feel a need for more collective nouns
To express gatherings, I need the words
For what I see in countryside or towns,
For companies, constellations of birds.
To start a sherbet of yellowhammer,
Just two, cocking a snook at clouds and rain,
And I saw and heard in their joyous clamour
The promise of sunshine, of springtime again.
And then on a field by Kirkstall Abbey,
A synod of jackdaws, and I feel blessed,
Shining and strutting, each one a hoody,
Eyes shifting for sparkle; a fallen priest.
A plumpness of wood pigeons beckons me
As I look for a new taxonomy.

Pastels, homage to Farrow and Ball

The sky is duck egg blue above the cars
And behind the big house across the way
Whose chimneys grandly reach and scrape the stars
Before they're put out by the brightening day.
I'm struck by these colours of dusk and dawn
Where no bonfires consume the bookend skies,
The fusion of soft colours, subtly drawn,
The slow sparking of the day, its closing eyes.
Sometimes these pastels move me more
Than the burning clouds or the hall-marked sea
And my spirit grows, fills the empty shore
Of what has been and what is left to be.
Promise is what I call my swelling heart
Rejoicing in a more reflective art.

City Stories

So city; will you show me who you are
And have been? Allow me to make a start,
To walk your streets, to stop and stare,
A poet's stethoscope to track your heart.
I will map the places where you and I have met,
The night-time square, the morning bike ride,
The gothic archway, the tower block set
With motorway booming at its side.
The club, the bar, the bright green of park
The filth and beauty of these urban lives
Where some feast on carrion in the dark
And hope is a train that never arrives.
If you trust me enough, I will try to tell
Stories of renewal, and tell them well.

Ordnance Survey

I knew then that I could still read a map
Unfolded on the table, countryside
Spread out, what I'd forgotten soon came back,
Lines and symbols, all in a simple code.
I trusted my cycle trip to memory,
The day was wet and windy, I'd no need
To wrestle this chart, strong breeze off the sea.
I could concentrate on my country ride.
And there it was, the fields, each rolling hill,
The villages, churches, woods and streams
Before me, and in my head pictured still,
The landscape of my memory, of dreams.
I looked for tumuli, for farms, and they
In actuality, before me lay.

Ave atque Vale:
with apologies to Catullus

Greetings now seem to be problematic
Folk are at a loss as to what to do,
I wheeze out 'Good Mornings', old, asthmatic,
Responses are different, some are new,
The shy, eyes blank, take refuge in headphones,
The friendly smile and cry out welcomes,
The chilly are chilly, no warmth in their bones,
But some are panicked, their hearts are drums
Calling out for flight or fight, they're not sure which.
The world has changed, certainties gone,
Unnervingly naked, not wearing a stitch,
Hoping for hope in the warmth of the sun.
Allow this old fighter to salute you well,
Hail to you, and if good-bye, fare thee well!

Dear Friend

This long separation has had no bars,
No barbed-wire fence between, keeping us apart,
We still share the day, the moon and stars
And always carry the other in our heart.
But we cannot yet hold and pull them close,
Feel their warmth and breath on cheek and skin
We have lost the humanity, the kiss
That we used to share, and linked one to one.
I wish to remember each single day
The enchantments of nature, the times of despair,
The being lost and finding a new way,
The navigating a world with no map to share.
But more than that, more than the sight
Of you, I wish to breathe you, hold you tight.

Something

I live in a city and by the sea
Where Wolds meet sky and clouds are fishing boats,
Luckily there's nowhere I would rather be
Than where I am. A blackbird's notes
Sound just as good in either place, as pure,
I am transported by the joy, the evening song
Perched on chimney pot or tree, and I am sure
That both places are where I belong.
But sometimes there is a special feel
To smaller city skies and the precious art
Of the blackbird chorister. I would kneel
To thank Something from my grateful heart,
But, of course I would feel quite compromised
Being cool, ironic, and civilised.

Crows

This might well be my final battleground,
A hilly lane in green, suburban Leeds,
A jousting bike, wheels hardly turning round,
Heart racing, forehead damp with sweaty beads.
It might all end with an electric volt,
Interior sparking that blows a fuse,
Fighting for air, and then the final jolt.
Falling off sideways, helmet over shoes.
I look at my final resting place, grass
Long and feathery, wild flowers duck and nod.
No one would notice me if they should pass,
The comedy if no-one finds my bod.
Fucked off, gone somewhere else, who really knows?
Bike stolen and carcass picked clean by crows.

Lincoln Green and Burmantofts

More than litter blows on these terraced streets,
More than graffiti paints each wall and door,
There are the tragedies of damaged hearts
And the strength of those who reached out for more.
Their stories haunt each brick and paving stone,
Road names tell stories of a former age,
Buildings weave tales of human blood and bone,
Their unheard histories, their stifled rage.
But what remains, though it might be faint,
Is the glorious garbage of the past,
And the swooping calligraphy of paint,
The love that bound their small worlds fast.
They trusted when each grubby day was done
Hope would rise in the east with morning sun.

Nearly Going to the Gym
with Dylan Thomas

I am now in hard training for old age
And if Dylan weren't late I would say to him,
'Come on mate, it's time to drop your rage,
Let us go gentle into Virgin gym'.
There was probably more than just a touch,
Last night, of whiskey shots, less a tasting more a flow
And promises to join me proved too much,
Hence me waiting, pacing, and his no show.
Finally a text from Dylan Thomas,
'go now without me into that good gym'
No punctuation not even commas,
And grammar seems to have deserted him.
'catch up laters, im really sorry bro'
This man's a poet but would you know?

Albert Morgan Nash,
1909–1984

Call across the valleys, parade-ground voice,
That I might hear you faintly, the static
Of the years between, hear you and rejoice,
Freed from the weight of headstone, emphatic,
With your country threaded and plaited through
Every rising cadence of your speech.
I would tell you how I am, and then you
Might take your turn, we have been out of touch.
But it cannot happen. I can only feel
You in some gestures, the language of my hands
And sometimes I hear in a quick reveal
The sounds of male voice choirs and marching bands,
And see you flickering in black and white
Faintly, before dissolving in the light.

High Tide: Kirkstall,
Leeds, 6.45am

I leave the gym and hear the sea is in,
A distant roar as the sky grows light.
My lamp bobs, flickers like a pin
In the slow dissolving of the night.
I will join the growing tide, the incoming wave,
Already poised to dive, a cycling fish
Among the pounding surf, I will be brave
As the waking city and the traffic clash.
I am momentary silver, food for shark,
Small fry leaping in the tidal roar,
Becoming larger in the retreat of dark,
As it lessens, I find that I grow more.
Each day I feel it in my early ride
The roar, the rise of the incoming tide.

Burley Park, Burley, Leeds 4

The pleasure of the city park, the chance
To breathe a little, for one's heart to slow
To see for moments in the quickest glance
A rural idyll, a bucolic glow.
In these stolen moments I can ignore
Other people there, the houses that crowd
Around the edge, I love it even more
Because of them. There is no shadow cloud
Can mar the peace these places give to me,
Although I have favourite times to visit them
And particular things to hear and see
There's little at any time I would condemn.
Perhaps the best is early morning when I pass,

Meat

At first I did not know what I could see
Carried by struggling men who bore their weight
From a lorry's doors, almost into me,
Half carcasses of ribbed and marbled meat.
I stood amazed at the architecture
Of bodies reduced, stripped of skin and fat,
Gaudí baroque and curves, the complete flair
Of function and design reduced to that.
I thought of cows in fields, and sheep on hills,
Philosophic munch of grass and flower,
Of liquid brown eyes, blood that pumps and thrills
Through live bodies, just something we devour.
What could I do this early summer's day;
What I have always done, just turn away?

Black Lives Matter,
Bridlington, 7th June 2020

The street is ordered, attentive and hushed.
The numbers warming my heart, giving me hope,
Hope for a future where folk are not crushed,
Their voices stilled by heavy knee or rope.
I stand with George Floyd, patient in the rain,
The 'I' has become 'we', tears sting my eyes,
Hope to witness Sam Cooke's a-coming change
Before another fellow human dies.
I think of all the lifelong nourishment
I've had, from Baldwin, Billie, Angelou,
Morrison, Langston Hughes, and what it meant,
I would bend creaking knees to all of you,
Then stand with Martin, George, Nina Simone
And all the nameless ones who now are gone.

Spring tide

This morning there is a surge, a spring tide
That's gilded the trees with buds, not yet green,
Though hawthorn on the path and to the side
Is hung with bright lichen, viridian.
The sun looms yellow above the hedges
And meadows where growth is still in hiding.
The sky not yet strafed by swifts, the edges
Of clouds soft, leaning over, confiding.
Mackerel scales reaching over the bay,
Arching from cliff across the sea to town
Telling us that changes are on the way,
Winter not quite knocked out, but on the ground.
The curlew strides and dips, everything
A jerky clockwork, celebrating spring.

Witness

I have become a witness to fences,
Their framing of banks of flowers and grass.
How they offer us subtle defences
Between the cliffs and sea, and fields and paths.
They run along in lines ahead and behind
Offering us the play of light and shade,
A wren perches to let its song unwind,
From behind it the sun a shining blade.
Now I look back at the fences I built
In different stages of my past
And see them clearly for what they meant,
Not impenetrable barriers that last,
Content enough to give them their full due
Not tear them down, just let the sun come through.

Petrichor

I can smell the rain, a battery scent,
Last quiver in the leaves, strange stillness now
As we wait in the garden for the slant
Of raindrops to fall, each one soft and slow.
Too soon for jasmine, this scent has power
To stir my senses and intoxicate,
Bewitching so that the world moves slower
As I sit out in the coolness and wait.
Singing stilled in the ragged apple tree
A blackbird flies across me to its nest,
I have no equal urge or need to flee
The first patter on skin and I feel blessed.
Later I go into the garden again
For the damp rich incense of after-rain.

Trails

Scribbles up above, circles of movement,
Sky writing slow dissolving into past,
We drive to the sea, their written comment
White against the blueness, East Riding vast.
There was a distant roar of planes retreating
But birdsong restored the music we hear
Watching the woods and meadows soft meeting
In this most hopeful, greenest time of year.
Later we climb down to lifeboat station
And up the slope to where the car is parked
We are replete with our daily ration
And I feel my imagination sparked.
The whisper trail a broken hieroglyph
To ancient religion and retold myth.

Queen Anne's Lace

In the week since we were last cycling here
Spring has turned to summer and all is green
In our whirl of wheels through morning air,
Plants have grown where none were seen,
Cow parsley has sprung up in shabby arrogance.
We chatter two abreast, sometimes single file
Leaving the city we ride in the present tense,
Our bodies and minds at peace for a while,
The canal is a mirror for the sky
Reflecting our journeying back to us,
New buildings either side the water lie
The city grows, extends insidious.
But just for now the rulers of this place
Are red campion and Queen Anne's Lace.

And now the butterflies have come

And now the butterflies have come at last
Late to the party but a final compliment
To spring. I rejoice in them, my blood moves fast
Amongst the drift of hawthorn blossom scent,
A connection to this place not felt so much before
From the first icy shocks of early spring
To the thousand greens, there may be more,
I see today and then this joyful fluttering,
Casual it seems around flower and leaf
And then I sense the earnestness of plan and scheme
Where the wild spaces offer some relief,
Catch the purpose behind this fleeting dream.
Today the Speckled Wood begins to stir,
Rejoice in every single sight of her.

Rosa Rugosa

The roses on the slipway to the sea,
Single petals around their scented heart,
Amongst the grasses and sand, bloom for me,
I am an extra with a walk-on part.
I slow right down and lean to breathe them in,
Talcum powder smell of childhood times
Of endless summers; the sea is touched by sun,
The sparkle of its blue; the answering gleams
Of May light on flowers banked around the path,
The rabbit holes, the gold of buttercups,
We walk into summer, feel a surge of truth,
Raise the glass of spring and put it to our lips.
Roses have simple enchantment, still felt
When we're challenged by what is difficult.

W. H. Davies:
I clearly stole your poem

I never understood 'the scenic route',
To amble slowly through the countryside.
It postponed any tasting of the fruit.
The prize of getting there, or just arrived.
But now I'd rather take the little lane
Or the long meander around the town;
On the slower journey I can regain
A sense of myself, that no rush could own.
So look, look, and look some more, watch with me,
See the sky full of murmurating birds.
Be witness to miracles on the way,
Take notes, take stock and you might find the words.
Remember, there's no prize for getting there
Relish the journey, slow down, brake and stare.

On Two Wheels in the Wolds, with apologies to W. B. Yeats

At first I do not recognise the sound
As I cycle the empty lane through fields,
And my eyes are reaching out, all around
To the greens and bright yellows of the Wolds.
And then I think it is the seashell breeze
Of a woolly hat pulled low over ears,
But it's a happy, busy sound, a tease
While I watch the fields for eccentric hares.
When I pause to take in the distant views
Then it stops, my body keeps ticking on
As if there's nothing left for it to lose
But might as well adventure while it can.
And I know what I cannot hear or feel
Is the bee-loud humming of each turning wheel.

Cycling to Central Park,
Manhattan, March 28th 2019

This is not Headingley. We're both on bikes,
The Hudson on our right and skyscrapers on our left,
Aiming for Central Park, no gears, no brakes,
Just fixed wheels turning, bobble hats aloft.
And I'm pedalling through all my years
Each one as sharp as the March sun for me
But there is no pain and no time for tears,
I'm seventy today, was meant to be
Cycling through Manhattan, a world of song,
Porter, Gershwin, Berlin and Ellington.
I am here, it's now, and nothing can be wrong,
I breathe in and out, it's my oxygen,
All the songs she sang to me as a boy.
Mine is the respiration of pure joy.

Punctured

I am pushing my bike, useless metal,
Reduced to this knackered geometry,
Along rich lanes where flower and petal
Light my way, but also where I see
The road deaths not counted by anyone
Apart from God, Nature, or whoever
Is keeping tabs on what we have done,
In making these short lives even shorter.
Dead rabbits flattened to fur mittens lie
With their guts a bloody smear, pheasant cocks
Broken feather machines, and there, still bright of eye,
A perfect pigeon upside down, no marks.
All this I see, as green spring and I are wed
While coat-hanger crows circle overhead.

Concertina –
a postscript to South Landing

I heard its wheezy leather lung, the jig
It played as I took the steps carefully,
My knees stiff with effort and with age,
To reach the little bay, the navy sea.
Then saw the old woman as her fingers flew
As if knitting a ganzie with cunning hand.
Playing squeeze-box shanties she made them new,
The busy sea waiting at her command.
We were the only human creatures there,
And I saw how swiftly those fingers moved
When she turned and talked, and began to share
How happy her late sea-side life had proved.
I still catch, if the tide runs high and strong,
Thin echoes of her concertina song.

Joy for ever

I had never once considered the thistle
To be a thing of beauty, just a thug
But I've changed my mind and this epistle
Lists the ways I love its gorgeous mug.
Stopping by a hedge late one sunny ride
I am caught by its purple vulgarity,
Saw poppies first, and then what grew beside,
Their silver architecture beckoned me.
Wren could have designed each dome and spire,
The complex pattern, prickling symmetry,
The vibrant unpacking of each purple flower,
A helter skelter, and now I can see
The strange wild beauty of this royal plant,
Heraldic, warrior-like and elegant.

Long-eared owl

OK, we did not see it. Though we saw a deer
Gambolling in a field as we drove by,
Where a fox had played the day before.
So when the ancient man stopped to say
That he had seen a long-eared owl
Siting in a tree, high up and saucer eyed
It was a gift, we walked looking up the while,
Hoping to see what he had spied
But the long-eared owl had left its tree
Sought a snoozing, sequestered space
And there was nothing for us to see
Apart from the generous beauties of that place.
The great pleasures of what might have been,
The hopeful joy in what we could have seen.

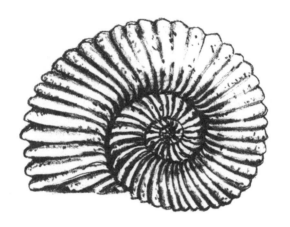

Wilsthorpe, one May morning

And we're among dunes and feathered grasses,
The sea, bright blue strip across drying sands,
Chickweed, snow-in-summer and wild roses
Make May joyful, birds sing in minstrel bands.
Dogs fly into the sea and out again
As if hermits from their cells unconfined,
And their owners share in this glorying,
Our dog just toddles and we do not mind.
But we must return to our Cowper lives
The pleasure of the sofa, cups of tea
But like the labrador that ducks and dives
We take back some wet magic of the sea.
Reminders of scent, each paint box shade,
The perfection of the morning brought inside.

Dog

When he was young he carried feathers home
Found fallen in the park, in puppy jaws,
These memories of flight, he relished them,
They delighted him for no apparent cause.
Sometimes now he searches amongst the trees
In our garden and scratches at the soil,
Emerging with an ancient bone he knows
He put there once, and now would reveal.
This canine contraband has a simple charm
For us like treasure found upon the beach.
In fondness I hold out a loving arm
To capture him, but he's beyond my reach
I wish him bones and feathers where he's gone
So when he sleeps and dreams, he's not alone.

Sea fret

At first the sea frets come spaced days apart,
There are sunny patches of in-between
He barely notices it, his head and heart
Not synchronised the way they've always been.
But Someone's moving things, he can't find his key,
Names have been stuffed in a drawer Somewhere,
Worries can assail him, Sometimes he doesn't know
Where he's going, when he's halfway up the stair.
Today he finds himself in the village shop,
No list, no bag, and he cannot recall
Why he is there, the penny doesn't drop,
He's on a clifftop, fearful he might fall.
The lighthouse siren wails, a warning shout,
As deeper fogs swirl in and blot him out.

Empty

Walking on the empty beach in 'summertime'.
We lost an hour last night, the world still snores,
The sea beats against the wall in endless rhyme,
We track the wet sand while the dog ignores
Us in the canine preoccupation of smell.
But we wade on the two of us regardless
Till he catches up as we know he will.
Why the world is so still he cannot guess
And it is a new world, though perhaps not brave,
We stride into, unknown days and weeks ahead,
We can only hope to know and to save
What is most precious, what we need.
The dog knows these things but he cannot tell
That love alone is what will serve us well.

Threnody

Phantom terrors break up my fragile sleep,
I wake to the cool of an April night,
Heart faltering in its efforts to keep
The machinery going until light.
I sit up in bed, reach to check the time,
Swing my legs to find slippers on the floor,
The dog wakes too, to him it's all the same,
Gets off the bed and beelines for the door.
I sit on a garden bench, the night sky bold,
Electric with stars and seaside clear
While the dog potters, and I feel safely held
By the subtle rhythm of music I hear,
It is the choral, eternal threnody,
The sigh-filled singing of the nearby sea.

Health and Safety

The slipperiness of everything,
The combination of wit and speed
Needed to deal with loss and suffering,
The handrails and ropes we sometimes need.
Our resources found wanting, not enough
To keep us afloat or hanging on tight,
We may lose our hold and tumble off
Into the cold tides of a winter's night.
But some things anchor us each to each
Give us direction where the ways are lost,
Strand us on the stones of an unknown beach,
Allow us space to count the actual cost.
To open the album of each bright day
Keeps the chilly darkness a step away.

In the bleak midwinter…

This is grim; it seems no end in sight
Though perhaps the darkest point is here,
The plumber will come, and this freezing night
Will die, and glow of morning reappear.
Until then we are reduced to a tribal dance
Negotiating the ice-cold shower,
Scott of the Antarctic would have no chance
But cometh the man when cometh the hour.
I ignore the shock to body, to heart,
And to ease the horror the plan we make
To introduce each single body part
On its own, wash, out again in a shake.
Cold-shower Hokey Cokey makes me shout,
'In out, in out, that's what it's all about'.

Duvet Dambusters

Ultimately this can feel like war,
Though I hesitate to use a tired term
High-jacked by some politicians for
Concealing ineptitudes which cause us harm.
However, lying in my midnight bed
With my partner and the sleeping hound
I am besieged by farting, sleep has fled,
Explosions and miasma hang around.
There is a puzzle to solve, if I should care,
Whence the explosions and whence the smell
I gingerly breathe in the sullied air,
Wonder where my inhaler is in this hell.
Dambusters below the duvet, above
The pong, from the two that I most love.

Affirmation

Our lives, that endless minute which we wait
For the washing machine door to ping, unlock.
So much, so much time, and then it's too late
And it's all over with the final click.
Will we see the cold wash was not enough
To clear the marks of a life fully led,
The stains are stubborn, recalcitrant, tough,
There are dried tears, old laughter and blood.
But it is too late. And always will be so,
No chance for fresh settings, it is all done.
The red light will go off, and then we know
What was a minute is now quite gone.
The door will open, other things will close.
So breathe in those perfect, transient joys.

The first yellowing leaf

With the first yellowing leaf, I can find
Myself wanting the journey and the death,
The last few weeks waiting on the wind,
The dying and the freeing, the chilly breath.
Because I am tired my faltering steps
Mimic old age, just a few seasons away
And I feel no urge for renewal, no hopes
For what remains of the year, mirrored by this day.
Autumn light with its apple cider taste
Is flickering and ripening across the sky
And letting go might seem like a waste,
The chance of change with each dying sigh,
So when you fly leaf I will not fly with you,
There is more to come, I embrace the new.

Chestnut Candles

Walking home after a shower of rain
Drops still fall from a fresh-dressed chestnut tree,
Below the paving stones glow and shine
Reflecting each candle blossom to me.
The city's spring season, I smell its green,
See hart's tongue clinging to the granite wall,
Seven decades of it in all I've seen,
And like the fern I'm still here after all.
With every breath that I breathe in and out,
My veins sing songs of joy and banish fears
Songs that bring in Spring with a happy shout
In the place that I have lived for fifty years.
And I walk in the sun on Yorkshire stone
Feeling the warmth and new life return.

Your continuing warm life

Your continuing warm life, bed sleeping,
Paws aloft, stomach warm and lightly furred,
Is so comforting, a way of keeping
A faith in life, death is once more deferred.
Sometimes it's just the presence of his life,
The heat of blood surging in each vein,
Which brings to my midnight fears some relief.
Life which seemed hopeless is good again.
One day, not far off and he will breathe no more,
The unknowing warden of my anxious mind
And I will lose this living, breathing store
Of what it means to be endlessly kind.
You are just a dog, but much more than this,
You have my heart and bring me peace.

Candle for Mags

I lit a candle in the ancient church,
Set it burning there with a borrowed flame
Amongst the ikon saints and high vaulting arch
To flicker for some hours in your name.
It was not a prayer, more memory,
And a signal for tears unshed 'til then.
The shadows it made had fallen on me,
You were gone, and not to be seen again.
There is a church not far from Larnaca
Where the candle has guttered and gone,
But the flame lives on in the hearts of us here,
Will burn bright for you as a benison.
You gave out such light in your few, short years,
And will shine clear and strong beyond these tears.

Caroline's story, whose skin this is…

after A. E. Housman

I have handwriting on my skin in blue,
Inked in, and etched through that integument
A sentence tattooed there, regretful, true
About a poet's loss and what it meant.
There's something sacramental in this weld
Between my skin and memory and brain.
The words I chose long since, for ever held
In silent ceremony, mute refrain,
Neat and cursive, drawn on my outer thigh,
Another's lines become my talisman.
So, if I wake at night and stir and sigh,
I can light the lamp and read them again,
Find once more in 'those blue, remembered hills'
The childhood innocence each word distils.

Jigsaw

So far above each tumbling, scrabbling piece
The upturned box, the tipping out of past,
Some piling, others falling into place,
Memories glitter amongst the gathered dust.
I move in closer, to start with edges or with sky?
The conundrums of a crowded life
And then the flowers catch my eye,
The passages of my life that gave relief.
Slowly I build them into a market stall
Of lilies and roses, of gaudiness.
A stripy awning covers them all
And I can almost smell their warm caress.
It may feel like everything has gone,
But piece by piece parts can be found again.

Pilgrims for Love

Pilgrims for love, we had travelled alone
On separate journeys, crossing foreign seas,
No compass to guide, no magnetic stone,
Just the stars' chilly glimmer in the dark skies.
Hearts were at low ebb, there were many storms,
Searching the unknown with flickering light,
Nothing to hang our hopes upon, only dreams,
Adrift and shaken in an endless night.
Then the sight of warmth in another's eyes
Was our landfall; the promise of a home,
A miracle of finding, no disguise,
The breath of new love, and no longer alone.
Pilgrims for love, finding the beauty and worth
Of becoming the other's one true north.

Respect to Otto, the much-loved Comedy Dachshund
2005–2021

Notes

Introduction
> 'gritstone' is a hard, coarse-grained, siliceous sandstone used for building materials.

'Winifred Holtby, Rudston:
A sixteen line sonnet, by accident'
> Winifred Holtby (1898–1935) born in Rudston, East Riding of Yorkshire, known mostly for her novel 'South Riding'.

'Ave atque Vale: with apologies to Catullus'
> 'Ave atque vale' from an elegiac poem by Roman poet Catullus, it means 'Hail and farewell'.

'Nearly Going to the Gym with Dylan Thomas'
> A little pastiche of one of the greatest poems in English, 'Do not go gentle into that good night'. By the great Welshman himself.

'Black Lives Matter, Bridlington, 7th June 2020'
> *George Floyd (1973–2020) killed when a police officer knelt on his neck during an arrest on 25th May 2020.*
> *Sam Cooke (1931–1964) singer, songwriter, civil rights activist. He wrote the song 'A Change is Going to Come'.*
> *James Baldwin (1924–1987) novelist, activist.*
> *Billie Holiday (1915–1959) singer, activist.*
> *Maya Angelou (1928–2014) poet, activist.*

Toni Morrison (1931–2019) novelist, teacher.
Langston Hughes (1902–1967) poet, playwright, activist.
Martin Luther King (1929–1968) Christian minister,
*   activist.*
Nina Simone (1933–2003) singer, songwriter, activist.

'Petrichor'
    Petrichor is the pleasant smell after rain.

'W. H. Davies: I clearly stole your poem'
    W. H. Davies – Welsh poet and writer whose most
    famous lines perhaps were:
        'What is this life if, full of care,
        We have no time to stand and stare.'

'On Two Wheels in the Wolds,
 with apologies to W. B. Yeats'
    Where I pickpocket 'bee-loud' from his poem 'The
    Lake Isle of Innisfree'.

'Cycling to Central Park, Manhattan, March 28th 2019'
    Cole Porter (1891–1964) composer and songwriter.
    George Gershwin (1898–1937) composer, pianist and painter.
    Irving Berlin (1888–1989) composer and lyricist.
    Duke Ellington (1899–1974) composer, pianist, and
    *   leader of a jazz orchestra.*
    Here the 'she' who sang is Billie Holiday, jazz singer.

'Wilsthorpe, one May morning'

A reference to the Romantic Poet William Wordsworth and his wonderful sonnet, 'Nuns Fret Not at Their Convent's Narrow Room'. Also a reference to the 18th Century Poet William Cowper, who wrote poems in praise of tea and whose long work 'The Task' had a section entitled 'The Sofa'.

'Threnody'

A threnody is a lament.

'Candle for Mags'

A benison is a blessing.

Larnaca is a city in Cyprus.

'Caroline's story, whose skin this is…'

A.E. Housman used the wonderful phrase, 'blue remembered hills' in his 'Shropshire Lad' poems.

'Pilgrims for Love'

The title appeared at the end of Milly Johnson's novel *My One True North* (Simon and Shuster, 2020).

Acknowledgements

Thanks go to:

David Robinson for his support and love.

Jo Brandon for her fine and subtle editing, often helping unlock what I really wanted to say, and making my writing shine.

Jason Edwards as one of my first readers, whose encouragement was, and is, boundless.

Milly Johnson for her generosity in promoting my poetry. A true friend!